Sports Illustrated KIDS
HOCKEY Shapes

BY MARK WEAKLAND

CAPSTONE PRESS
a capstone imprint

Sports Illustrated Kids Rookie books are published by Capstone Press,
1710 Roe Crest Drive, North Mankato, Minnesota 56003
www.capstonepub.com

Library of Congress Cataloging-in-Publication Data
Weakland, Mark.
  Hockey shapes / by Mark Weakland.
     pages cm.—(Sports illustrated kids. SI kids rookie books)
  Includes bibliographical references and index.
  ISBN 978-1-4765-0225-0 (library binding)
  1. Hockey—Juvenile literature. 2. Shapes—Juvenile literature. I. Title.
  GV847.25.W43 2014
  796.962—dc23   2013015392

Editorial Credits
Anthony Wacholtz, editor; Ted Williams, designer; Eric Gohl, media researcher;
Eric Manske, production specialist

Photo Credits
Eric Gohl: 28–29; Newscom: ZUMA Press/Tony Bock, 22–23; Shutterstock: Tumar, 18–19,
Vaclav Volrab, 1; *Sports Illustrated*: Damian Strohmeyer, 10–11, 12–13, 20–21, David E.
Klutho, cover, 2–3, 4–5, 6–7, 8–9, 26–27, Robert Beck, 14–15, 16–17, 24–25

Printed in the United States of America in North Mankato, Minnesota.
032013   007223CGF13

Hockey is a fast and furious game. Shapes fly by in the blink of an eye. What are the shapes of hockey? **Let's get in the game and find out!**

circle

A bird's-eye view shows players ready for action. All games start at the center **circle**, where players battle for the puck in a face-off.

Huddling players crowd around the goalie, forming a **triangle**. The players gather as a team to get excited before the game.

Triangle

Square

College hockey helmets have face masks made of metal wire. The wire is shaped into **squares** that are too small for a hockey puck to fit through.

Rectangle

A hockey goal is a familiar shape. The mouth of the goal forms a large **rectangle**. To keep the puck from going into the goal, a goalie throws out his arms and legs. He blocks the shot!

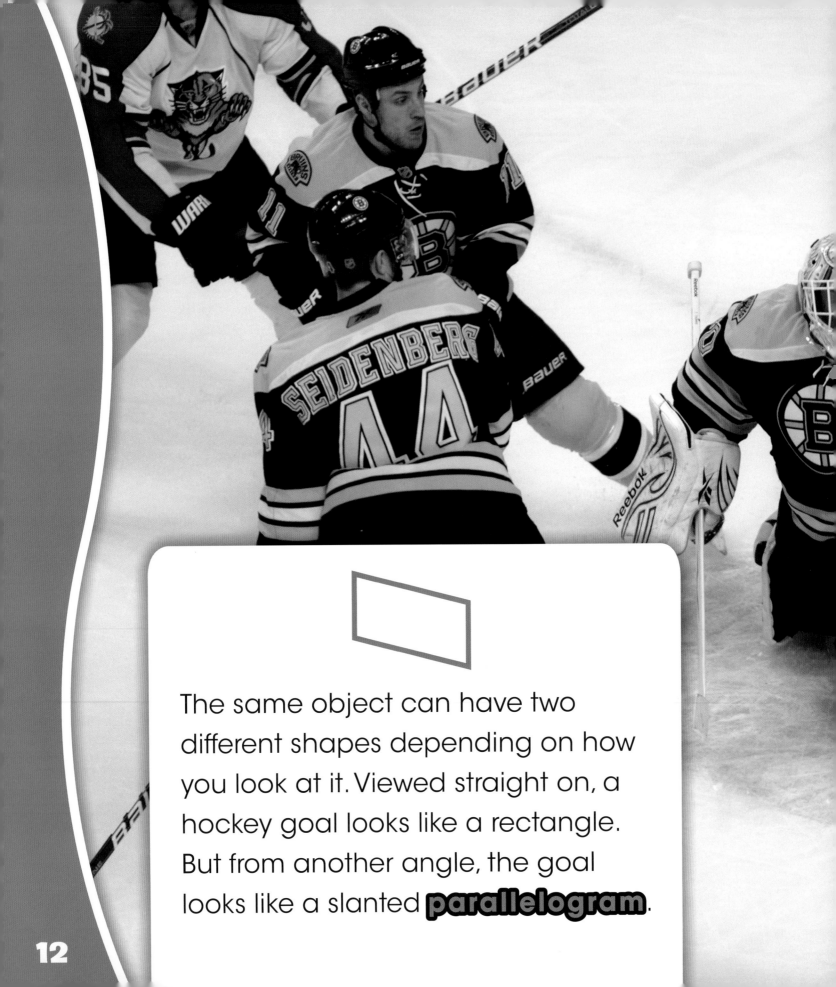

The same object can have two different shapes depending on how you look at it. Viewed straight on, a hockey goal looks like a rectangle. But from another angle, the goal looks like a slanted **parallelogram**.

Parallelogram

Trapezoid

The area behind the net is shaped like a **trapezoid**. A trapezoid has four sides, but only two of them are parallel. The goalie can only touch the puck behind the net if it's in the trapezoid.

Pentagon

A **pentagon** is a shape with five sides. Can you see the white pentagon on the goalie's jersey?

A goal's net shows dozens of **diamonds**. A diamond is a shape with four sides. It is also called a rhombus.

Diamond

Hockey jerseys display many shapes. Do you see a red **oval**? How about the white oval? There's even a tiny black oval in the middle. When players cheer and raise their arms, it's easy to see the ovals.

Oval

Star

Hockey games are full of shapes, points, and lines. A happy hockey player shows his **star**. Each star has five points and 10 lines.

Hockey pucks are three-dimensional shapes. They have height, width, and depth. Each puck is a short **cylinder**. Stacking several pucks creates a tall cylinder.

Cylinder

Cube

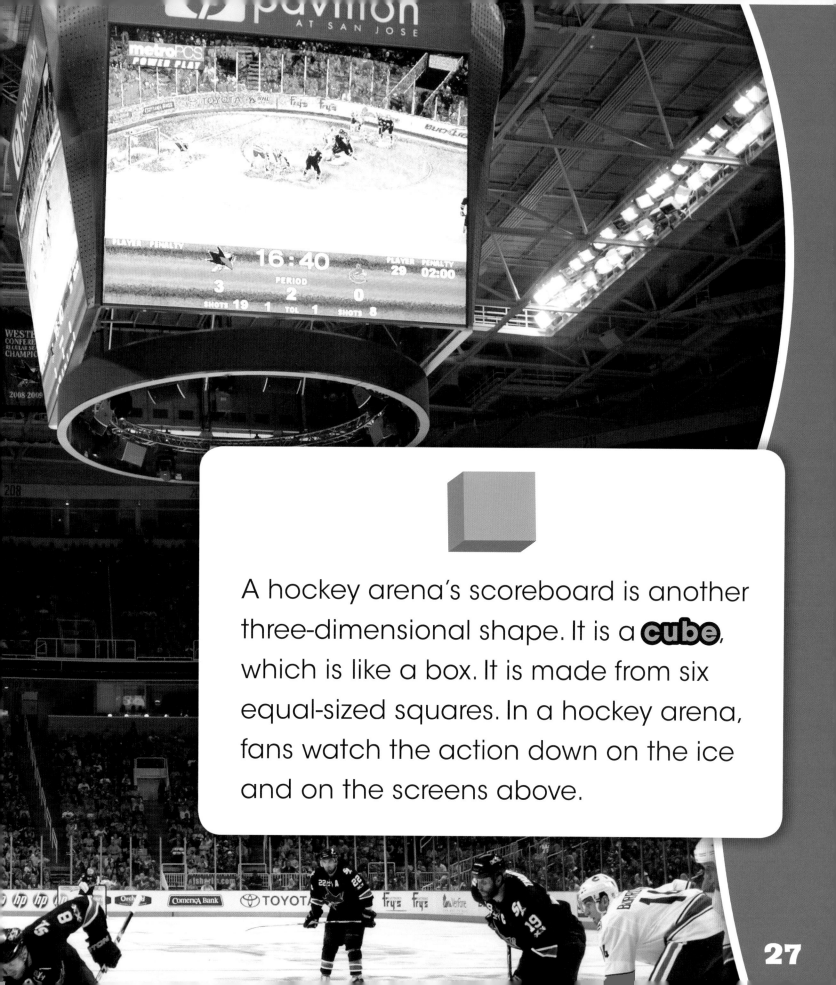

A hockey arena's scoreboard is another three-dimensional shape. It is a **cube**, which is like a box. It is made from six equal-sized squares. In a hockey arena, fans watch the action down on the ice and on the screens above.

For hockey players, the puck is a very important shape. So is the goal. But there are many more shapes to find at the hockey rink. What hockey shapes do you see?

Glossary

arena—a large area that is used for sports or entertainment

cube—a three-dimensional shape with six square sides

cylinder—a three-dimensional shape that has flat, circular ends and looks like a tube

jersey—a sports shirt worn by athletes; jerseys often have the team name, last name, and number of the player

parallel—being the same distance apart at all points

parallelogram—a four-sided shape in which the opposite sides are parallel and equal in length; a rectangle is a parallelogram

rhombus—a four-sided shape in which all sides and opposite angles are equal; a rhombus is also called a diamond

three-dimensional—having three dimensions: length, width, and depth; three-dimensional is often shortened to 3-D

trapezoid—a four-sided shape that has only one set of parallel sides

Read More

Frederick, Shane. *The Best of Everything Hockey Book.* Sports Illustrated Kids. North Mankato, Minn.: Capstone Press, 2011.

Jordan, Christopher. *Hockey Shapes.* Plattsburgh, N.Y.: Fenn-Tundra, 2011.

Napier, Matt, and David Milne. *I Spy with My Little Eye: Hockey.* Ann Arbor: Sleeping Bear Press, 2011.

Internet Sites

FactHound offers a safe, fun way to find Internet sites related to this book. All of the sites on FactHound have been researched by our staff.

Here's all you do:

Visit *www.facthound.com*

Type in this code: 9781476502250

 Check out projects, games and lots more at **www.capstonekids.com**

Index